After the Tax Sale

What happens after you attend a tax sale in
Mississippi

David Lewis

ISBN   1453860665
EAN-13 9781453860663.

Business and economics
Investments
Real Estate
Tax Sales

Table of Contents

Topic   Page

1. Introduction.   5
2. What happens immediately?   6
3. But wait. Done right?   7
4. No, you can't.   9
5. That Monthly thing.   11
6. Last day, or is it?   13
7. Date, not deed, gives ownership.   15
8. Okay, now what?   18
9. Title search.   20
10. Be sure to take notes.   22
11. Bring them flowers.   23
12. Title search. [yes, again, and again.]   24
13. What? Another place to go?   25
14. Who noticed?   26
15. Can you read a map?   28
16. Meat and what?   29
17. Out on the range.   30
18. I hate math.   32
19. Go look at it.   33
20. You better be sure.   34
21. Find a wheel.   35
22. Is that a house?   36
23. Who's there?   37
24. The diplomat.   38
25. Oh, no, what did I buy?   39
26. E P who?   40
27. The dump in the jungle.   41
28. Your new neighbors.   42
29. Be nice, they bite.   43
30. Get their names.   44
31. There may be a pearl in that slimy oyster.   45
32. Remember Sanford.   46

33. Decision time. 47
34. Wholesale or retail. 48
35. Legal aid. 49
36. The banker. 50
37. The broker. 51
38. The insurance salesmen. [There's two of them] 53
39. Try it yourself. 55
40. Your sign. 56
41. Answer the phone. 57
42. What price? 58
43. What bay? 60
44. Form letters. 61
45. A pretty face. 62
46. A weedeater $^{(TM)}$ doesn't get it. 63
47. Dump truck and front end loader. 64
48. The city says. 65
49. As is. 66
50. An ad in the paper. 67
51. Sure, they'll buy it. 68
52. Back to the neighbors. 69
53. What about the original owner? 70
54. Better get a lawyer. 72
55. Opinions. Now what? 74
56. Let's go to court. 75
57. Do it right the first time. 78
58. If anyone answers, hang up. 80
59. Judgment day. [You hope] 82
60. Don't forget policy. 83
61. It's developing nicely. 84
62. Now for the sharks. 86
63. Tell it like it is. 87
64. The fine print. [Theirs and yours] 88
65. Your hot little hands. [not till it's there] 90
66. Charts and things. 92
67. What taxes? 93
68. More taxes? 96
69. Are we done yet? 97
70. Don't just sit there. 98
71. Not again! 99
Summary. 100

1.
Introduction.

Many people have asked me to write this book. Chancery Clerks, Tax Collectors, and tax purchasers have all requested it, although for different reasons. Chancery Clerks and Tax Collectors have repeatedly answered questions from uninformed or misguided tax purchasers. Unfortunately, they themselves seldom understand all the procedures of the tax sale. Many tax purchasers realize the need for more information, but there is no other single source except, possibly my book, "An Introduction to the Mississippi Tax Sale," which explains the sale, but perhaps is more involved than what they need. Here then, is what usually can be expected after the tax sale is over.

2.
What Happens Immediately?

First of all, you pay for what you bought. That is, most people do, but there are always a few who get nervous, and realize that they have committed themselves to buying something that they know little about. And maybe for a lot of money. Throughout the State, lots of people do this. But the law says that the Tax Collector is supposed to locate you, and if you don't pay, then it's off to court, where you will pay in one way or another.

For those of you who pay, however, sometimes the Tax Collector will give you a certificate that describes what you bought and how much you paid, right when you pay. But in many of the larger counties where as many as several thousand parcels may sell, it may be a few days before they are able to print the tax certificates, and they will usually mail them to you.

The various Tax Collectors may have different policies as to what form of payment may be accepted. Some accept personal or business checks. Others do not. Some may require cash or secured payment. Some may accept a credit card as payment. Be certain to determine this information in advance with each different Tax Collector.

In either event, once you have paid for the parcel, title passes to you immediately but the original owner retains the right of possession, and may redeem for two years. Technically, you now own it. But don't get too excited yet. There's more to come.

3.
But Wait. Done Right?

Has there been a mistake? Did you really buy what you think you did? Did the Tax Collector really sell what you think was sold? Tax sales have been around for over a hundred years, and most people should know how to do it by now, right? Right, they should. But they frequently don't. While there are numerous rules and procedures to follow, there are also some common mistakes that will void the sale of some or all of the parcels sold.

The most common in many counties is the sale of a parcel containing more than 160 acres, without first offering it for sale in no more than 160 acre sections. Most Tax Collectors fail to recognize this when they are selling the property, and thus sell it as one piece without at least offering it as prescribed by law. The sale of this parcel will then be void.

There are sometimes more than one tax owed on a property, due to such as a charge-back from the state, a cleanup fee, or prior tax not collected. When this occurs, all taxes on one property must be combined and sold to only one tax purchaser. If this is not done, then each sale to a different person would be void.

Another mistake frequently made, is to refuse to take a property owners money if they wish to pay their taxes during the sale. This will void the sale of that property. Even if the property owner waits several months or more, the Board of Supervisors will have definite grounds to void the sale. They will probably give you back your money, but it may be awhile. You may even have to formally request it.

Every Tax Sale must be advertised in a local newspaper each week for two weeks. Failure to do so will void the tax sale.

A mistake also occurs when there is a reason why the Courthouse can not be used for the sale. The tax sale must be held at the Courthouse, or other site designated by the Board of Supervisors. If the sale is held in a location other than that designated, the entire sale is void.

And if you want another stupid reason for voiding the entire sale, how about this? The sale must be held on the first Monday in April, or the last Monday in August. How about if they held it on the fourth Monday in August when there were five Mondays? Right. The sale was void.

In the coastal area of Mississippi, we are obviously prone to hurricanes. Katrina provided another reason to void an entire sale. Since the hurricane hit on the day of the sale, many sales were canceled or interrupted and needed to be postponed. This was acceptable, and there is a procedure for doing that. Unfortunately, not all Tax Collectors read the Mississippi Code, and therefor, did not properly advertise the new date for the sale. Once again, sorry about that, but the entire sale could be voided. Some Tax Collectors have failed to advertise the initial sale in the newspaper. Guess what happened? Most of the time, though, whatever you bought is yours.

In fairness, it should be pointed out that in many of the smaller counties, when a new Tax Collector takes office, a completely new office crew is also hired. They may have little knowledge and experience with the correct procedures of the tax sale and there is little means for them to find out. Caveat emptor. Let the buyer beware.

4.
No You Can't.

This is one of those terribly misunderstood points about the tax sale. Yes, perfect title passes to the tax purchaser at the tax sale. HOWEVER, no, you can't set foot on the property that you just bought. In fact, you are probably the only person who, without any further warning, would be guilty of trespassing if you did enter upon the property.

Let's look at this point. To begin with, although you receive perfect title, it has two important loopholes. First, the original owner has a period of two years in which to redeem the property. If the property is redeemed, it is retroactive back to the day of the sale, as though the sale never took place. Therefor, it acts as if you never bought it. Understand?

Another right that is retained, is the right of possession during that two-year redemption period. The original owner may occupy the property during that time. It may even be sold, although all the purchaser receives is those same rights for the remainder of the two-year period.

Tax purchasers are not considered to be innocent purchasers entitled to perceived value received. They are considered to be knowledgeable investors. This means that by purchasing at the tax sale, you realize all these things ahead of time. You've heard of ignorance of the law, being no excuse. Well, here it is again. Only this time, that statement has definitely been upheld by the Mississippi Supreme Court.

As stated in the beginning of this section, you can not trespass on any property you purchase at the tax sale, and if you do, you are subject to prosecution, perhaps without any additional warnings such as a no trespassing sign. You will be liable to arrest for trespassing. No ifs, ands, or buts. You WILL be liable for arrest. Don't go onto the property.

At the end of the redemption period, if the property has not been redeemed, then you can get a tax deed, and enter upon the property, always assuming there was nothing wrong with the sale.

Are you getting excited yet about your new purchases? Keep reading. There's more bad news to come. And maybe a little good news too.

5.
That Monthly Thing.

Tax sales seem to be a reasonably good place to invest your money. For those who agree, and purchase several dozen or more parcels, the welcome or unwelcome news, is that each month or so, you receive a check from the Chancery Clerk for the taxes that were redeemed in the prior month. You get back the amount of taxes you paid, plus interest at the rate of one and one half percent for each month or part of a month. If the parcel had been sold in August, and not redeemed until August of the second year, you would receive interest for 25 months. Obviously, the longer time you hold the certificate, the more interest you get.

The interest is not compounded. It is figured as simple interest at the rate of 1 ½ % times the number of calendar months or part thereof. At the end of each year, you will receive a Form 1099 from the Chancery Clerk's office for all of the interest paid to you for that year.

Although it should not be necessary to point this out, sometimes things are confusing, so let's make it perfectly clear that once a parcel is redeemed, the tax purchaser has no further right, title, or interest in that property. None. Sometimes a parcel is redeemed and we either don't remember to make note of it, or even occasionally, we don't get the refund for it. Before taking any actions regarding a property that you think has matured to you, be absolutely certain that the Chancery Clerk says that it has forfeited to you. Every once in a while, an error does occur. Be very careful.

Two things here. The sale is in the form of an auction, and the bidding starts at the amount of taxes and penalties owed, and goes up from there. Anything you bid over the base amount is called excess. And you don't get it back. Ha, Ha. No, you don't. Now, you may wonder why anyone would bid more than they could get back. There are basically two reasons for this. First of all, with interest rates low, a person could bid several percent over the base amount, and still average better than by putting the money in the bank.

The second reason is that many people are risking that the property will not be redeemed, and that they will therefor be getting the property for little more than taxes. Or at least so they think. More about this to come. Regardless, the excess overbid goes to the county. In some counties, the excess has amounted to over two hundred thousand dollars. They get to keep it too. They thank you for participating in the tax sales. Your help with the budget is greatly appreciated.

6.
That Last Day, Or Is It?

For the most part, by the time the two-year redemption period has about ended, almost all of the parcels will have been redeemed. There are many different strategies that people use to purchase tax certificates, but as a rule, from ninety to about one hundred percent of the parcels are redeemed. The average is probably about 96%.

At the close of business on the second anniversary of the tax sale, the redemption period expires. Let's make this point absolutely clear.

Many people think that the redemption period is three years. It is not.

Another point is that the redemption period is for two years from the sale, and has nothing to do with the date of the sale during the year that it ends. Sometimes the sale for a particular year will be held before the redemption period ends, and sometimes it will fall afterward. Actually, because the last Monday in August will always be August 25th to August 31st, the dates will never both be the same.

Many people think that if the sale was held say on the 27th of August, it would mature at the end of the day, on August 26th, two years later. It does not.

The law ignores a part of a day. Therefor, on whatever day the tax sale was held, that is the date of the ending of the redemption period. And a person may redeem their taxes anytime up to the close of business that day.

The next day, a person can not come in to redeem the parcel. They no longer have any right, title, or interest in the property. Supposedly. There are several exceptions to this. To begin with, if the correct sum of money to pay the redemption amount is mailed with a postmark of that last day or earlier, it counts as having been paid on time, even if it arrives at the Chancery Clerk's office several days late. There are two points here. It has to have been postmarked on or before the last day of redemption, and it must be for the correct amount. Another exception is that if a person pays with a check which is later not honored, and they are unable to make it good before the redemption period has expired, they have lost the property. Every year, some that were redeemed at the last minute were done with a bad check. Too bad, they lose it.

Because of the problems stemming from these issues, most Chancery Clerks will not issue a tax deed for at least ten days after the last day of redemption. And, of course, you probably won't be notified by the Chancery Clerk until they prepare the checks for the previous month's redemptions. They might not even send any notice to you.

To recap this, you will have no way to determine accurately, whether a parcel was redeemed or not, during the last few days, unless it was paid in cash.

Unfortunately, the main reason that the original owner's interest may not be ended, is due to a lack of understanding of the rules and/or, carelessness. And that almost always stems from the response of the Chancery Clerk's office. They get a lot of misguided help from the sheriff's office also. Probably over 99% of the reasons that a tax sale is voided, or otherwise overturned by the court, is through the actions, or lack of them, of these two departments. The US Postal Service also provides their share of obstructions. More to come about this important problem

7.
Date, not deed, gives ownership.

There is a great deal of confusion about this next subject. Let's try to settle a few issues. If you don't understand, don't feel bad. Many attorneys and judges don't understand this part either.

First of all, let's look at Mississippi law as it applies to the filing of deeds. Basically, if you purchase property from someone, it does not officially belong to you until you file the deed. Once the deed has been filed and recorded, it is almost useless. If the Courthouse does not burn down or get flooded as in the recent hurricane, then you will probably never have a need for your deed again. As a direct opposite to the chapter title, it doesn't matter when a deed is signed, it does not take effect for most purposes unless and until it is filed.

On the other hand, if it is not recorded, then you do not own it. Period. Normally, the attorney who handles a closing, will file the deed for you, but not always. Sometimes they forget. The important thing here is that if it is not recorded, then you don't own it.

Well, how does this apply to our interests in this book? The issue revolves around the tax deed and a list. The tax deed or Clerk's conveyance is almost useless, except that it serves as proof of ownership, which should give the right of possession, and which you can show to a neighbor, former owner, or sales person. Now, just why is it useless? To understand this, it is necessary to understand the workings of the tax sale itself.

As has been said, immediately after the property sells at the sale, perfect title passes to the purchaser. This change in ownership is sent by the Tax Collector to the Chancery Clerk, in the form of a list that has all the necessary information. This list serves as a deed. Since many counties routinely sell several thousand parcels at each tax sale, imagine what a chore it would be to draw that many individual deeds! Instead, the law says that this list serves as a master deed. And the Chancery Clerk is supposed to record it in the same manner as any other conveyance. Well, that is what the law says. Somehow, it doesn't seem to have the same import as a regular deed, but that is another story.

The tax deed only acts as a visible proof that you own a property. It is a representation of that list provided by the Tax Collector. And the date that it becomes effective, is as of the end of the two year period after the tax sale, not on the date that it is officially issued. Remember, that list was filed two years ago, right after the tax sale, and it became enforceable in the same manner as a regular sale, on the second anniversary of the sale. This issue has been confusing to many, but after considering just how the sale works, it becomes a little easier to understand.

If you don't need to file a tax deed to put the parcel in your name, just how does it happen? Who knows? Actually, on the second anniversary of the tax sale, the Tax Assessor should, after waiting the few days for checks to clear, and mail to be delivered, automatically place any unredeemed parcels in the name of the tax purchaser. Don't hold your breath. Almost without exception, they will never do this. In fact, in many counties, they will probably not even do it if you file your tax deed. They should, but good luck. Many Tax Assessors will add tax purchasers as a double claimant or as an additional owner. There is no such thing. They are completely wrong. You are the new owner. Period. In some counties, it will be an almost impossible task to get them to realize this.

This whole point about ownership after a tax sale matures, is completely misunderstood. Many people who work in the Chancery Clerk's office and the Tax Assessor's office, still believe that you do not have good title until you receive a judgment in your favor following a suit to confirm the tax title. They may even tell you and others that all you have is a tax interest or that you are something called a double claimant. At that point, there is no such thing as a double claimant or only a tax interest. Now, telling you this is not going to make it right. They will still continue to believe what they will, and you probably won't be able to change their minds, but we keep trying.

It is a bit humorous to listen to them tell you that the tax title and even the tax deed is not any good, when the only reason that that might be so, is if they personally did not do their jobs. More on this later too.

The important points here, are that on the date of the maturation of the sale, which is at the close of business on the second anniversary of the tax sale, title to the parcel automatically becomes absolute in the name of the tax purchaser. But it will be several days before this can be determined. There is a tax deed that is issued by the Chancery Clerk, but it is not necessary for complete title to pass to you. Additionally, there will probably be some difficulties in dealing with officials. Play it easy.

8.
Okay, Now What?

If, after several days past the ending of the redemption period, you discover that a parcel or perhaps several parcels have forfeited to you, then what? Just what can you do? Well, that usually depends on just where the property is located. Your tax certificate, or even your tax deed, when you get it, may not give you much of a clue as to what you bought. It might be the property next door to where you live, or in some remote section of the county.

If it is only land, with no building on it, it will almost always be difficult to know its location. How come? Well, you are used to locating someplace by its Post Office address. This, however, is not its legal description. And that is why it becomes more difficult. The deed is filed according to the location of the property, and by its legal rather than Post Office address.

If you are fortunate enough to have purchased a property that lies in a town, then it probably is filed under the subdivision that it is in. Some of these subdivisions are so old, that you will not have heard of them. They are only thought of as an area of town. If your parcel is one of these, you are in luck. Now, you are probably thinking that you don't feel lucky. Even if the parcel is within the town limits, the subdivision doesn't necessarily help you. What to do? Well, the Chancery Clerk's office or the Tax Assessor's office, will have a map that will point you right where you want to go. You can locate your newfound property by the parcel number. You can then find the name of the owner of the neighboring parcel, and look them up in the phone book. That will give you an address, and you can take it from there.

Here comes the unlucky part. If your new property is located in the country, then you will have to do some more work.

For the time being, let's forget about where the properties are located. There is another thing that needs to be done. At this point, you must decide which to do first, either go to look at the property, or to run a short title check to see what the status of the property might be. Title issues may override the value of the property. On the other hand, the property may not have enough value to justify putting any money or effort into it.

We have done it both ways, and have found that we wasted our time by doing one or the other first. Sometimes, there is something such as a lien on the property, which is for more than the property is worth. Sometimes the property does not seem to have much value. It may be very small, or oddly shaped, or have a ditch running through it. Before you can determine what to do with a parcel, it is important to both physically look at it, and to run a title check.

9.
Title Search.

So, let's look at a title search first. Perhaps the best advice here, is don't. Don't try to do it yourself. Now, personally, I hate "How-to" books that tell you to have a professional do something. But believe me, there is a very good reason for having someone else do your title work. Mistakes happen. And when they do, they can be expensive.

For instance, recently we confirmed title to a piece of property. The title company did their own title search. They missed a deed. The title insurance company had to pay us over a hundred thousand dollars. If we had done the title work, we would not have gotten a nickel, and, in fact, would have been out several thousand dollars. And I have done occasional title work for over thirty-five years. I could perhaps have done this myself. It is fortunate that I did not.

Notwithstanding the foregoing, it is important to know if there is at least an obvious problem. The most suitable solution is to hire someone to do a title search for you. They normally charge about seventy five to about a hundred and fifty dollars for a 31 year search. Note that this search is not adequate for a confirmation suit that is done correctly. If they turn up anything negative, you can decide whether to pursue it any further.

It is, however, frequently difficult to locate someone to do the title search on tax property. Mostly this is for two reasons. First of all, there are a number of notices that become critical to the title issue and most abstractors are just not that familiar with the rules. Secondly, since most tax properties will eventually have to have their titles confirmed, and the law requires a 60 year search for that, it involves more work.

When you can get a title search from an abstractor on a tax title, they usually charge about double and still seldom get all of the notices. This leads to another expense, but one that will probably be necessary in the long run for any parcel that might be of some value. Almost without a doubt, you will need to go to court to confirm that the title to your new property is good.

Obviously, this will normally require an attorney, and they will usually have an abstractor who will do the title research.

10.
Be sure to take notes.

If you try to do your own title search, be sure to take notes. It could be quite important to review a certain transfer or lien at a later time. Another difficulty is that there are frequently errors in the description or location of the property. It is not unusual for a deed to have been drawn that scrambled or left out a line of the legal description.

Almost without exception, any competent attorney will refuse to accept a title that has such an error. It will need to be corrected. Of course, another problem would arise when you go to look for it. It is obviously important to have a correct location.

If you look at a series of deed transfers, they may still not all contain the same descriptions because many times only a portion of the property is sold at a time, such as in the case of a large tract of land which is broken up.

Obviously, this can be very complicated, and a good title search may point out difficulties that would be cost prohibitive to overcome.

11.
Bring them flowers.

You will probably be spending a lot of time at the Chancery Clerk's office. You probably will ask more than your share of questions. You will probably make a nuisance of yourself. Those who work there, do the best they can to help people, but they don't always have the time. Be polite and appreciative of the help they provide. And sometimes they really do deserve flowers.

12.
Title search. [yes, again, and again.]

Whenever we do a title search, it seems that something odd turns up. Actually, almost half of the titles have at least something minor wrong with them. That may not sound too good, and it isn't. Nevertheless, that has been our finding. Usually the problem is not too important and can be corrected, but it does have to be done. As we said, a good example of something that might not be apparent immediately, comes to light when you research back deeds. It is not unusual for there to be a difference in the descriptions on the deeds.

Sometimes this can be a major headache. Check them very carefully. Another typical error comes when the original purchaser of a property is not the one who sold it on the next deed. This happens frequently when a surviving spouse sells a property, especially when a death certificate and court approval are not included or referenced in the deed.

Sometimes a descendant or remarried spouse with a different last name, may have signed a deed with no supporting documents referenced. In cases like these, clear title may be very difficult to obtain, and could be quite expensive. Before you invest too much money, this is the type of information that you should get from a qualified title search.

13.
What? Another place to go?

Sometimes a town will have their own tax sale. When this happens, you must check both the County and City records. Incidentally, the County tax deed takes precedence over the City deed, and if both are issued, then you may have to go to court to clear the title, but you will probably include that in the suit to confirm the title and remove clouds.

It is particularly important to also understand that while a property may be located several miles outside of the limits of a city, it may still be in a school district served by that municipality. And if the city collects its own taxes, then they probably also collect the school taxes for those properties that are located in the county, but still within that municipal school district. This happens very frequently in those areas where a municipality collects their own taxes, so be certain to investigate.

14.
Who noticed?

Now, here we get to the place where all the mistakes get made. There are four simple things that have to be done, and they seldom are. The first thing is that the Chancery Clerk must determine the present owner of the property as of 180 days prior to the expiration of the redemption period. Since the deeds are filed in their office, it would seem to be a simple matter of looking up the current owner and of course, any lienholders. Unfortunately, if the property sold at some point back between then and the tax sale, they frequently fail to place the correct name in the notices.

Next, the Chancery Clerk must determine the location of that latest owner, and both give the sheriff a letter to deliver in person and mail a copy of the letter. If unable to locate the former owner after two tries, the Clerk must file an affidavit to that effect. This locating and mailing a copy of a letter, and having that letter served by the sheriff, must be completely accomplished within the period of 180 days to 60 days before the end of the redemption period. Recent court decisions may indicate that an affidavit must be filed for each time they are unable to locate the owner.

Lastly, at least 45 days before the sale matures, the Clerk must advertise in a newspaper, the list of parcels that are about to forfeit.

These things seldom are done correctly. If you decide to file suit to confirm your tax title, these should be critical to the case. Basically, you must find out who was sent a notice, and when. There may be a little ambiguity as to when the owner should receive the notices, but the courts have accepted a time of sixty days as a minimum. It is almost never done on time. In fact, many times it is not done at all. When that happens, if you attempt to confirm the title, you should lose your case.

As must be obvious, this ought to be one of the first things you need to determine. Some errors are acceptable or perhaps correctable, but you will probably end up with little or nothing for your efforts.

15.
Can you read a map?

Every piece of property in the County is located on a tax map. In town they may be easy to locate, but out in the country, it may be almost impossible. Unless you understand how to read a map, it will be very difficult to accurately locate many rural parcels.

A shortcut that may save a lot of time, is to look up the owner on each side and maybe across the street. Then, when you get to the approximate location, you can check mailboxes to determine a little closer, where your new property might lie. A good investment might be to purchase a detailed county or tax map, although they are sometimes rather high priced.

16.
Meat and what?

Most properties that are not in a municipal area, and some that are, are located by a process called metes and bounds. This is partly simply saying that one side of a parcel is adjacent to, or bounded by that belonging to someone else. In the past, people seldom moved, so it was quite common knowledge where the boundaries of properties were, and who owned them.

Today, however, those people may be long gone and forgotten. Yet their name may remain as part of the land description. Imagine what fun it is, trying to locate a parcel bounded on all sides by unknown persons and perhaps a street whose name has been changed.

17.
Out on the range

Additionally, most of the country has been divided into sections of one square mile. In order to keep track of each section, they are numbered, and grouped together. There are supposed to be 36 sections of one square mile each, in every group. Sometimes, though, due usually to terrain problems such as swamps and other impassable obstacles, there may be some odd shaped sections, and even more than the usual 36 to a particular group. Each group is described as being so many groups North or South of a line called a Township, and East or West of a line called a Range. Briefly, a parcel might be described as being in Section 9, Township 7 South, Range 15 west. Most counties then, will contain about 4 to 6 groups east and west, and about the same north and south.

The MDOT puts out a highway map for each county that locates all of the sections by number and gives a pretty good general idea of a parcel's location.

Now let's get back to that thing called a Section. As we said, there are usually 36 of them and they are usually one mile square. It is common practice to divide the sections into quarter sections labeled NE, NW, SE, and SW quarters, and then to further divide those into quarters, making blocks that are ¼ mile in each direction. Since there are 5,280 feet in a normal mile, and thus only 1,320 feet on the edge of a ¼ of ¼ of a section, no place is too far from something that has a definite location. In fact, all of the Section corners have or at one time had markers placed by the government surveyors.

At first glance, this might seem pretty difficult to understand, but let's review it and see. First of all, the complete State has been surveyed usually into one mile square blocks called sections. A marker has been placed at each corner. These sections have been numbered from 1 to 36 and collected into groups.

Surveyors use the distance from one of the corners to locate any property in that section.

18.
I hate math.

Where it begins to get difficult is when the description reads so many degrees East or South, etc. And most all surveyed properties will be described that way. Still, that is how any property in the state can be quickly located down to one square mile or less. The dimensions within that section will take a bit longer, but the better able you are to read a map, the quicker and easier it will be.

This is going to be a little complicated, but let's give it a try. A typical property might be described as starting from a point called a POB, or point of beginning. It then might say E 10 degrees 32 minutes S 120.4 feet thence N 04 degrees 21 minutes E 212 feet thence W 11 degrees 17 minutes N 121.7 feet, thence W 86 degrees S 214.3 feet to POB.

Basically, this is saying go Eastward, but slightly South by 10 degrees and 32 minutes for a distance of 120.4 feet. Then turn and go almost straight North but a little bit West, by 4 degrees and 21 minutes, for 212 feet. Then go West but slightly North by 11 degrees and 17 minutes, a distance of 121.7 feet. Then turn and go West but Southward by 86 degrees 214.3 feet . Then you will be at the starting point.

A map has 4 directions, each 90 degrees apart, and each degree has 60 minutes. Then you must be able to judge approximately what portion of that 90 degree difference is reflected by the 0 to 90 degrees in the description. Notice that in the above example, the last direction was W or West but then 86 degrees South. That 86 degrees actually makes the direction almost due South. Enough. If you understand, great. If not don't worry, it may come to you, or if necessary, you can hire a surveyor.

19.
Go look at it.

Finally, it is time to go look at your newly acquired land. There is no way to be certain about it's value without seeing it, so you will need to physically locate the property before you know what to do with it. While this may seem to be a simple assignment, there may be a number of difficulties.

One thing to bring with you is a camera. Take pictures. Make yourself familiar with all the details of your new property. It is easy to forget some detail that may affect its value, and pictures can help solidify its points in your mind. They are also great for some sales literature.

20.
You better be sure.

One person who worked in this business, was told to change the lock on a newly acquired house. He had just completed drilling out the old lock, when the owner arrived. Imagine the fun when the man was told that he was on the wrong street.

In a similar situation, I bought a lot and after a few months, drove by it and saw where a contractor had mistakenly started to build a house on it. That made for a quick sale, but it could have dragged out in court. Be absolutely certain that you have the proper location before doing anything with the property.

21.
Find a wheel.

Perhaps you have seen various people using a stick with a wheel to measure accurate distances. In this business, that is a very valuable tool that can be purchased for beginning at about twenty dollars. Usually, I can pace off up to three hundred feet or more fairly accurately, but for accuracy, I always carry that wheel gauge in the trunk.

If you have properly located a parcel on the map, you need to also locate a landmark that you know you will be able to find out in the field. Road intersections, bridges, power lines, and similar landmarks can be much more readily determined than most properties. Then you can measure the distance to the middle of your property. That way, you will have some room for error to either side of the parcel.

Obviously, it is critical to accurately measure the distances both on the map, and on the ground. More than once, we have just driven by, and estimated the location, only to learn later that we were off by a hundred feet or so. Be very careful.

Another difficulty comes with locating the rear of the property. No matter how well you think you can sense directions, it becomes next to impossible to wade through brush and weeds for any distance and still maintain an accurate direction. Perhaps the best thing to do here, is to get a general overview of the property, and leave the exact corner points for a surveyor if it is really necessary.

22.
Is that a house?

Most parcels turn out to be vacant lots. Sort of. But sometimes there is a house or building. Sometimes it's difficult to tell. Remember, many times it will have been several years since anyone paid taxes on the property, and it will frequently have been vacant all that time. Many such structures will actually make the property worth less, because they will have to be demolished. More on this later.

23.
Who's there?

Then there is the house that is obviously occupied. Now what do you do? First of all, are you absolutely certain it is the right house? Even so, what do you say to the occupant? This is a constant problem for tax purchasers.

Perhaps the best advice here is to turn around and go back to your research. Double check and even have someone else go over your research. Check the telephone book and the city directory if there is one. Try to determine just who might be living there. If there is no homestead exemption on the property (you can find that out from the Tax Assessor), then it is possibly a rental unit. Some counties have much of this information available online, making it much easier to do your investigating.

When you are absolutely certain that you are at the correct property, then what? At some time you will have to contact the occupant.

24.
The Diplomat.

No matter how certain and determined you are, be diplomatic. There might be a very good reason that it is occupied. If so, you may need to go to court to settle your claim, and in most cases, you will lose. More about this later, also. Another point here, is never talk to a minor who lives there about these matters. There are too many ways for that to cause difficulties.

When you do talk to someone, either take notes immediately after the conversation, or record the conversation. You may not be able to use the recording except to refresh your notes, but it is surprising what is actually said versus what you think was said a few days later. Be as accurate and pay as much attention to the exact wording as you can remember immediately after talking. If possible, use exact quotes.

Another point here is the eventual disposition of the property. We sell a high percentage of the parcels we get, back to the original owners or to a relative or neighbor. Whomever you talk to may be your eventual purchaser. Don't antagonize them.

25.
Oh, no, what did I buy?

This section serves to exemplify two points: talking with neighbors, and buying something without properly investigating it. Recently, we were offered a parcel that had accrued to another tax purchaser. We investigated and discovered a valuable commercial site. Then we asked the neighboring owners, and got a slightly different impression. The sight had previously been a gas station, and apparently the gas tanks were still in the ground. And they were leaking. If that is not enough said, then you need much more than this manual.

Discussing things with the neighbors can sometimes be of considerable value. Obviously, researching about the parcel before you buy it, can also make a considerable change in its obvious potential value.

26.
E P who?

Perhaps you have heard of those government agencies with
three letter names such as FBI, CIA, IRS, and very important
to unsuspecting tax purchasers, the EPA. Can you imagine
the expense of removing the huge leaking gas tank, and the
surrounding dirt, and testing how far the gasoline had seeped?
We did not purchase that excellent property.

An additional word here. It is our understanding that
anyone anywhere in the chain of title may be held responsible
for cleanup expenses by the EPA and some other agencies. If
you inadvertently purchase a property that falls into one of
their categories, be prepared to obtain the advice of an
attorney.

Obviously, when taken with the Supreme Court's ruling
that you are a sophisticated and knowledgeable investor, you
may want to do a great deal of research before purchasing any
property at the tax sale.

27.
The dump in the jungle.

Most of the time, we don't have such a headache, but it can even be worse. Most urban areas want vacant lots cleaned and mowed, and they will charge you if they have to do it for you. Remember that by the time you get the property, it will frequently have been after several years of neglect. And just visualize someone getting hurt on that property.

As soon as the property forfeits to you, you need to view it and make immediate plans to accomplish any necessary maintenance.

If you acquire very many properties, or even one fairly large one, be prepared to spend a considerable amount of time and energy as well as money to bring it into shape to sell it at the most advantageous price.

28.
Your new neighbors.

One of the most important things to do while inspecting a new property, is to talk to the neighbors. They have all kinds of information and are frequently the most logical buyer. They may be able to tell you what happened to the original owner. They may know about someone who has long been interested in purchasing it.

They may at least think that they know about where the property boundaries are. Unfortunately, this is one of their least valuable information gifts. They are almost always wrong. Listen for clues, but do your own measuring, or hire a surveyor.

Regardless of your feelings about it, they are going to be a part of the package in one way or another. If you are fortunate, they may 'keep an eye on it for you.' They may even mow the grass, sometimes for little or nothing, just to keep up the neighborhood.

29.
Be nice, they bite.

On the other hand, they may be tired of seeing the eyesore next door, or angry about someone getting nice old Mrs. Brown's property. Now they have someone to focus on. It can become a very expensive time. Diplomacy and quick thinking are quite important here. Many times you can turn negative feelings to positive ones by trying to identify what it is that they want.

If they are angry about someone getting the property, you may have to steer them into concern that the owners or heirs did not attempt to assume their responsibilities, and that at least now, someone will be taking care of the property.

If they want the property cleaned, try to get it done as soon as possible. Tell them that it your desire to see it looking better also. It is not unusual to locate at least one of the neighbors that wants to maintain a lot. They want the neighborhood to look good, so they sometimes even offer to do it for free, but don't count on it. In fact, because of potential lawsuits, you may want to do the work yourself, or hire a contractor.

30.
Get their names.

But like I said, many times they will be the ones to purchase that property. You may want to get their names and write them a letter.

Since many properties have little value by themselves, it might just be that those neighbors are your only potential sale. Even if you don't talk to them, get their addresses and look them up in the phone book.

An important detail particularly with city lots, is that they used to be quite narrow. Today, building codes frequently require a much wider area. That makes a lot between two older houses almost useless except as a lawn or garden for one of the adjacent property owners.

There is another point here. They may call you about the property. If you have already talked with them, they will expect you to remember them. It makes them feel better if you remember their names, which is sometimes hard to do after a few weeks or months. Keeping that information in a file may serve quite well.

More than once, a neighbor that we sold a property to, later purchased another that we contacted them about. They can be very important potential buyers.

31.
A pearl in that slimy oyster?

One of the most difficult things for most people to see is the value in a junk covered lot in a less than desirable neighborhood, or a dilapidated house. Remember though, someone lives in that neighborhood, and they may just think that that house or lot is just what they or a relative needs.

Over the last forty years, one of the most glaringly obvious points in real estate valuations has been the fact that even seemingly minor blemishes have drastically reduced the selling price, considerably beyond the expense of repair.

An overgrown, weeded lot in an area, will almost always sell for several thousand dollars less than if it were clean and mowed. Yet it might only take a few dollars to clean and mow it.

Houses are even worse. If there is an obvious need of repair, many people will not even consider purchasing it, regardless of the price. The remainder will always drastically lower the offering price.

There is always a trade-off between selling it as-is, and putting more time, effort, and money into it, but at least a little improvement will almost always result in a faster sale.

32.
Remember Sanford.

Remember Sanford and Son. He sold junk that others found a use for. It does not matter whether or not you like a property, but only whether or not someone else does. We have sold dozens of properties where we would never consider living, but someone else obviously would. The point to remember here, is that everything has a value. That value may even be negative, but in almost every instance, there is someone who will be willing to purchase it. You just need to find them.

Time and again, we have undervalued properties that others found somehow desirable. It is difficult not to, because much of what eventually forfeits, gives at least the first impression of junk.

Here we also need to interject another point. We are not attempting to create an inflated value, we are simply trying to see the property as someone else might. A problem that frequently occurs is that when we attempt to use a real estate broker, they take one look and decide that it is not worth their time. When that happens, you can either try to educate them, or get another broker. If they do not believe in your project, then they will not sell it. There are a number of additional issues with real estate people that we will cover later.

33.
Decision time.

At some point, you must decide what to do with your newfound bargain. Unfortunately, this is where procrastination takes over. No matter what you decide to do, the key is to at least do something.

The issues include what immediate steps need to be taken to secure, clean, mow, and protect the property. What ongoing maintenance will be needed? What improvements would be cost effective to increase either the sales price or the sales appeal? Who are the potential buyers and why? Somewhere in all this, is the realistic question of what the property is worth.

The bottom line here is that all of these decisions have to be made, and a plan for how to dispose of it must be drawn. When you find yourself with not just one or two, but perhaps several dozen, as we do each year, the need for some sort of concerted effort becomes much more obvious. But even with just one, nothing gets done unless someone does it.

34.
Wholesale or retail.

Should you auction it as is? Should you do any cleaning and upgrading? Should you get a better title? It depends mostly on the value and the strength of your title.

We have sold properties for more than we thought they would bring. We have sold many more for much less than what we felt they were worth. The keys here have usually been the questions of turnover speed, further investments vs increased profit, and first and foremost, the title.

There is another point here, which is to not fall in love with the property. We have sold dozens of things at much less than full value. Sometimes it is simply the most expedient to dispose of properties at whatever price we can. That may not sound too intelligent, but some property may just never sell at anything close to what you think it is worth. Or, and this is very frequently the case, there is just an extremely limited number of potential buyers.

There are numerous reasons for selling below what you may think is the fair market value. The biggest hurdle though, is actually managing to sell it. There are many ways to sell even large numbers of properties fairly quickly, but they don't normally yield too high of a sales price. We'll also cover some of that information later.

35.
Legal aid.

Now it's time to decide how valuable the property is. Even though the tax title is supposedly good, it is not usually perceived that way, and you will probably have to have the title confirmed by the court. The reason that tax titles are not usually accepted without further legal action is generally because of the faulty procedures of the sale itself. Or more precisely, those of the Chancery Clerk's office.

If the property appears to have sufficient value, it will be time to perfect the title. To be practical, this is where you will need an attorney. There are two aspects of the title that will need review and an informed opinion. As we said, about half of the titles examined, had an error. While most of them were of a relatively minor nature, some were not. An opinion from an attorney can save you a great deal of time and expense.

The second reason for an attorney's opinion is that of the tax sale process itself. Was everything accomplished in the prescribed manner? If not, how will that affect your case? Seemingly minor issues may have legal ramifications that will transform a potentially valuable property into a legal quagmire that could cost thousands of dollars.

Let me give you just one example. Several years ago, we purchased a quitclaim deed from the authorized signer for a partnership. Sometime later, we were surprised that the title company would not issue a policy since not all of the partners had signed. An attorney might have reviewed and caught this, but if not, his insurance company would have had to pay to make it right.

36.
The banker.

Some times you can sell a parcel without confirming the title, but most banks will not loan money against it. That is not to say that they will not loan money on a property with only a tax title, only that they probably will be cautioned by their attorneys not to. The bottom line here is probably the credit rating of the borrower.

Although it may not be able to be financed, that is about the only area of concern if the potential purchaser is only going to use the land for a garden or say as an extension of his neighboring lawn. Of course, the original owner might still file a suit to reclaim the property, but if the purchaser has no more invested than the original purchase price, and is willing to assume that risk, usually based on a substantially reduced sales price, then there are few additional reasons for concern.

37.
The Broker.

Most Real estate brokers will not handle unconfirmed tax properties, and sometimes they actually cause more harm than good by their distorted views on tax properties. Check carefully about their understanding of the process.

Here again, a little knowledge can be a dangerous thing. We have had real estate salesmen tell potential buyers that all they were getting was a tax interest, not a real deed. This is a very common interpretation. Even people who work in the Chancery Clerk's office have some such perverted ideas. The fact is that there is no such thing as only a tax interest. The tax title is a perfect title unless and until it is overturned or modified by a court of appropriate jurisdiction.

Of course, since most tax sale procedures have not been followed completely, the end result if someone brings it to court, will be that you lose.

Nevertheless, a knowledgeable real estate broker is an asset that should be searched for quite diligently.

One procedure that we use, and which should only be attempted with a broker who is familiar with the tax sale process, is to place the property for sale with the proviso that a marketable title will be provided within 90 days. That allows us to not invest any more into a parcel until we have a contract, and then we initiate a suit to confirm the title.

The real estate broker can be of use in several ways. Besides having an office that people can go to, and recognizable signs, and a perceived removal from the actual buyer during negotiations, they have one additional advantage. Today, many people make use of the internet to search for a suitable property. And that is where your broker can do something that you usually can not. They can place your parcel on the multiple listing service. That does two things. First of all, it places your information in the hands of all of the local real estate agents, but it also normally allows individuals to access most of that information on the internet.

Our real estate brokers sell only about half of what we list. The remainder is sold through other brokers, some of whom have clients that saw the listing on the internet, but preferred to go through a broker that they knew.

A good broker will help you sell properties, but a bad one may prevent a sale. If you are not absolutely confident in your broker's knowledge and understanding of the tax sale, and cannot educate him, change brokers. Or do it yourself.

38.
The Insurance Salesmen.
[There's two of them]

Once you have gotten a perfected title, you may want to insure yourself against any future problems. That is normally done with a title insurance policy. Your liability is something else. You may also want to insure against someone suing you for injuries.

When you have a property that has a title that appears to have no potential concerns as to its legitimacy and completeness, many companies will undertake to insure it against any future claims. They generally specialize in only this type of insurance, called a title insurance company, or they may be an adjunct of an attorney's services.

This is called title insurance, and normally costs about $50 plus another $4 for every thousand dollars in value that they place on it. Notice that it is the value that they place on it. Here we have a running battle with several interpretations of existing laws.

Briefly, you cannot insure something for more than its value. (except someone's life, perhaps) The difficulty here lies with the first question that the insurance agent asks about it, which is 'how much did you pay for it?' For most normal properties, it would be a reasonable and necessary point since it would likely be worth whatever you paid for it. Obviously, that does not apply in our cases.

It is sometimes impossible to persuade the agent to insure a property at what you simply say is its fair market value. This is another instance where a real estate broker can be of considerable value to you. They can produce a market analysis to show its potential sale price based on its similarity to other comparable parcels. Such a document, usually called a CMA (comprehensive or comparable market analysis) or a similar name, can normally be used as an acceptable guide towards its insurable amount. The real estate broker may charge you for this, or if he thinks you may generate enough business, may provide it for free.

Now for the other insurance agent. Remember that weed covered, junk strewn lot? What happens when someone gets hurt there? For that matter, even a manicured lawn, perhaps wet with dew, may cause someone to slip and fall.

To protect yourself against these claims, it may be desirable to obtain a liability insurance policy. This insurance is normally included as a part of your homeowner's extended coverage policy. It (the liability portion) can be spread in what is referred to as an umbrella coverage, to other buildings and particularly the vacant lots that may forfeit to you.

The cost is all across the board. We have had several houses and vacant lots added to the liability coverage on our house, for less than a hundred dollars extra. We were quoted less than a thousand dollars for a policy to insure over 70 parcels. On the other hand, even with no claims, the premium on a policy tripled in one year.

The bottom line here, is that you may want to secure one or both of these policies, and that the conditions under which they will issue a policy may vary considerably. You must be able to provide the necessary information and guidance in order to obtain the most satisfactory results. Remember, you probably will at least eventually, be more knowledgeable than many agents about what you want to do in these circumstances.

39.
Try it Yourself.

When it comes time to sell it, you may want to try it yourself. Also, many brokers don't want to handle inexpensive properties, so that may be your best option. In fact, for practical purposes, it may be the only option in smaller areas where there are no real estate brokers who either want to, or are knowledgeable enough to properly handle these types of properties.

But is that so bad? What exactly does a real estate broker do for you? Well, let's not forget that CMA. But aside from that, they have several additional advantages. They first of all remove the responsibility for the complete process from you. They frequently have knowledge of persons looking for distressed real estate, or perhaps building lots, and can contact them directly with information about yours. They can place a sign on the property and process all inquires. They provide a sort of intermediary in the negotiating process. They have walk-in traffic to their office, which might result in a sale of your property.

All of those are distinct advantages. But sometimes, it just isn't feasible. Then you have to do it yourself. Some of the things normally handled by a broker, can be easily accomplished by the individual, especially after developing the necessary contacts.

We regularly put up signs, advertise, write letters, make phone calls, close the sales, and draw the deeds ourselves. We also use real estate brokers and attorneys to do most of those things. Normally, it depends on how much we feel like doing.

40.
Your Sign.

You can purchase a 'For Sale' sign and put your phone number on it very cheaply. Walmart sells them for less than a dollar. If you acquire very many properties, it might be suitable to have signs printed, perhaps including your phone number. There are a number of companies available on the internet that produce signs for a very reasonable cost.

Some signs can be mounted on a wooden or metal stake and pounded into the ground. Others might be nailed to a tree. Remember that if someone can't see your sign, it isn't going to do much good. We normally bring signs that have already been fastened to a stake, as well as loose signs with a hammer and nails in the trunk of our car. That way, we can put up whichever type is appropriate.

We usually put the sales price on lower valued property signs. This seems to draw more responses, but many are from those who are only curious.

We have seen signs nailed to telephone poles. Don't do it. It is against the law in most instances.

A problem that occurs with most signs is vandalism. You need to drive past your properties regularly. If the grass needs to be trimmed, or the sign straightened or replaced, be prepared to take care of it as soon as possible.

41.
Answer the phone.

Rarely do we get more than 10 calls about a particular property. Normally we get less than five or six. You should have all the answers ready if someone calls. You don't usually get too many calls, and each one may be the person who eventually buys it.

If you or whoever answers the phone, does not have the answers handy, you may lose the sale. This cannot be stressed enough. As was just pointed out, you seldom get even six calls. That is all that will be in the group that includes the one who eventually buys it. If you lose a potential customer because of a problem on the phone, you may have just lost any chance of selling it.

Some people use cell phones exclusively, and these make contacting someone relatively easy and convenient, but if that contact does not result in getting the information that they want, the people likely will not call back. If you are going to place a number on your sign, consider using a telephone where the information about the property is stored.

42.
What Price?

Value depends on all of the regular factors as well as how good your title is. A real estate broker may be able to help with the comparable market values. That should produce an approximate concept for the asking price. Unless you are extremely familiar with the local real estate market, a good system is to ask your broker what the property should be listed for, and how much to expect the sale price to be.

This, however, can produce a difficult situation. On the one hand, if the broker's estimate is lower than what you think it should be, he is not likely to portray confidence in that higher price that you might require him to offer. That may result in a totally lost sale.

Or you may harbor resentment because it sells for too low of a price. Or worse yet, you may not accept a lower bid that happens to be in the range of what the broker feels is acceptable, but you do not. This also might result in not selling at all.

When you and your broker can not quickly and honestly agree on a property's value, it may be best to not give him the listing. Or, if you develop enough trust in his judgment, then go with what he says. That's one of the things you are paying him for.

We just resign ourselves to accepting what he says, and more times than not, his listing estimates are higher than ours. And the sales prices usually are comparable also, so we are normally better off following his advice.

However, one time a broker suggested a sales value of approximately $6,000. We felt that it was very low. We did not list it with him. We later sold the lot for $18,000. This was an instance of miscommunication, more than broker error. He was thinking of one part of a subdivision where the lots were selling for that price. We were thinking of a different part of the development where the prices were quite higher. This should serve to point out the value of having your broker look at the specific property before agreeing to a listing price.

43.
What bay?

We have sold dozens of parcels on E-bay. For properties you think might sell for under about $10,000, that may be the fastest and most suitable avenue. As in most other efforts, it is still necessary to do at least a minimum amount of work in order to expect a reasonable return.

There are a number of concerns with advertising a lot for sale on the internet. In fact, most of those concerns apply to almost any means of advertising something for sale. Let me illustrate by an ad that we placed for the rental of an upstairs unfurnished apartment with stove and refrigerator. People called and wanted to know if it included furniture. One person was all ready to make an appointment to see the unit, when I happened to review its features. He said he didn't want an upstairs apartment.

No matter how complete, obvious, and accurate you attempt to make your ad, there will be some who see only what they want to see. They will email and call you about things you already covered in the ad. What is even more important, particularly with unconfirmed tax properties, is that they will contact you sometimes more than a year after the sale, to say that you did not tell them that it was a tax property. Or, they may not pay any back taxes that become due, and may in turn, lose the property to someone else. They will then blame you. Keep records of your ebay ad and all communications with the purchaser.

In almost all cases, it is better to have a picture with your ad. If possible, more than one might be even better.

They offer a quick sale at a fair price. Check it out.

44.
Form letters.

Perhaps the cheapest and easiest means to begin
negotiations to sell a property, is to mail a letter to all of the
neighbors. For the less valuable properties, and many of the
more expensive ones, they may be your only potential buyers,
but the fact remains that for certain categories of real estate,
the neighbors and possibly some investors make up almost
100 percent of our sales. Send a letter to each of the
neighbors and anyone who has expressed an interest. Offer
them a firm price for a limited time.

However, there is one important thing to consider here. No
matter what you feel that the property is worth, your desire is
to sell it, not to hold it. We always request that a broker or an
individual buyer submit any offers. We have had properties
listed for $20,000, that we eventually sold for $7,000. If it
doesn't sell at one price, then perhaps it is not worth that
much.

It may look more professional to have letterheads printed,
although most computer generated ones are probably quite
acceptable. While you are thinking about it, get some
business cards. It seems that situations always arise where
someone expresses an interest in one of our properties and
requests a card.

Let's get back to the letters. We have about 10 different
versions of cold calling letters that we send out. Some have
very minor differences. But we have one to cover most
situations. It not only makes it easier to know what to write,
but prevents most mistakes that might be accidentally
included. They are on the computer and only require changes
to the property description, the price, and the names.

45.
A pretty face.

Almost everything looks better cleaned up. The value of a neatly mowed lot is usually much more than a weed and junk covered one. There are basically three reasons for maintaining a lot in good condition. Obviously, the neighbors and the city or county may have some very deep concerns about overgrown and trash covered lots. It is normally much cheaper to take care of it yourself, than to let the government do it. By the time they do, the neighbors will likely be quite unhappy also. And remember, they are frequently your potential buyers.

The other two reasons are that a more attractive and appealing lot both enhances the value and increases the likelihood of a sale.

Along the line of those last two points, a house that has a broken window, needs to have the trim repainted, and badly needs the grass mowed, will first of all, not likely sell at all, and secondly, will only do so at several thousand dollars under its otherwise market value. This happens time and again. Even though the cost to repair the window, repaint the trim, and mow the grass, is probably relatively minor, the sale price will always be much lower than the cost of repair and cleaning.

We have seen people decide not to purchase a house because the carpet or the walls were the wrong color. What is the chance that they would purchase something that needed any work?

46.
A weedeater™ doesn't get it.

Here is where the responsibility factor comes in. Owning a property requires several obligations including paying your share of the taxes and maintaining the property.

We saw a house that required a dump truck, a front end loader, and many hours of work to clean the yard. A vacant lot required several trips to the dump. One lot that had been cleared a few years before, had 40 foot tall pine trees.

Sometimes you may need to have land cleared by a bush hog. If you don't have the equipment, it is sometimes available for rent, or there are people who do that type of work. Whether you decide to do the work yourself, or to hire someone, get it done as soon as possible. Remember, you normally want to sell the parcels you get, not keep them forever.

47.
Dump truck and front end loader.

As we said, many times the only sensible solution is for you to hire someone to clean and haul off trash from a vacant lot. You may want to try renting the equipment and doing it yourself, but it becomes a major chore very quickly.

The key point at this juncture, is to not be overwhelmed by the immensity of the task. One of the most difficult things to do is to make a decision about something with which we are totally unfamiliar. The task seems magnified.

We normally do one of three things. We procrastinate. We continually put off making a decision. Obviously this serves no useful function.

Or we chip away at the problem. We bring over our little lawn mower and perhaps a few trash bags. Then we simply get bogged down in the immensity of the task.

Eventually, we may do what we should have done first. Stand back and review exactly what needs to be done. Then determine how best to accomplish that. Then take a deep breath and DO IT.

48.
The city says.

Unfortunately, most vacant land has been sitting idle for several years before you get it. Probably the local authorities are going to want something done with it very quickly. There is an established procedure for having the city clean a property. Except in cases of extreme circumstances, it takes several weeks, and the property owner needs to be notified. He is then given a period of time in which to effect the cleanup, or to negotiate for a longer time.

Eventually, the bottom line is that a person will have to either clean the lot or let the city do it. Here we have to make a decision. Sometimes the city can do it for less than you can, but don't hold your breath. Still, you could let them solicit bids and then, you might possibly be able to clean up before they let a contract.

In the event that the city does clean the lot, they will bill you for it. Depending on the time of the year, they may add it to your tax bill, or they may put it with the next year's bill. Unfortunately, there is another alternative. They may seek to have a judgment rendered against you that they will try to enforce by placing a lien against you rather than the land. If this happens, you need to contact an attorney. With a judgment against you, you cannot sell a property with a warranty deed, and it will go against your credit rating. Try not to let it get to that stage.

49.
As is.

Most of what we sell is sold as is, but that doesn't mean that we don't at least try to spruce it up a little. Remember, the buyer's first view will set the tone for his buying price. To begin with, he might just not consider it further if it looks less desirable. Or he will certainly offer less than he otherwise might.

There is still the other aspect of 'as-is.' How good is the title? We sell almost everything with a quitclaim deed. Whether we have only a shaky tax title, one that appears rock solid, or even a judgment issued from a suit to confirm the title that in many ways is better than a warranty deed, we do not convey title by that warranty deed.

If we do not have what is considered a marketable title, that is, one that any knowledgeable person would, upon review, find generally acceptable, we sell the property in an 'as-is' condition, no matter what it looks like physically.

The key point here is the fact that even though we are selling as-is, we will still usually receive more money and/or sell it quicker if some cleanup is performed. It is sometimes important to do whatever it takes to create a sale.

50.
An ad in the paper.

An ad in the local paper or neighborhood shopper type paper may lead to your best sale for distressed type properties. Many people have used this simple method to sell from one to several hundred properties. That is what your local real estate broker does. You can too.

There are books written on the subject of producing ads that work. Perhaps the best thing is to look at the ads in your local paper. What seems to work for you? Those weekly shopper papers are normally much cheaper, and seem to work well for the lower priced properties.

Grouping several of your properties together, may result in lower costs. They sometimes also result in the sale of all or at least a large portion of the parcels in the ad, to a single purchaser.

51.
Sure, they'll buy it.

Over the years we have heard hundreds of people say that they were going to buy something. Maybe next week, or when they sold something else, or just maybe as soon as they can arrange financing. Don't hold your breath. Get it in writing with a deposit, or don't count on it.

Our children still talk about one old sounding man who would call periodically to say that he would buy the house as soon as he sold his corn crop. It was sad, funny, and annoying, but it happens.

We sometimes take a deposit to hold a property, but about half of the time, the people do not return. That is not something that we like to do, so we regularly try to discourage people from that practice.

By talking with the potential buyers, you can usually assess whether they will be able to complete the sale. Don't let your desire to sell it, override your common sense.

This happens with about half of the properties, so be ready to explain your procedures to the callers.

Another thing that always happens, is for people to ask if that is your bottom price. We always try to give the impression that it is, but that if they want to make a formal offer, we would look at it. They rarely do. The trouble here is that once you quote a lower price, then that word gets around, and now that becomes your asking price. And you still haven't got a bid.

52.
Back to the neighbors.

Go back and talk to the neighbors again. Usually someone will buy the property if the price is right. Be prepared to negotiate, or just to take whatever offer they do make. If it is a firm offer. Remember that you can't keep lowering the price, or they will simply wait until you give it away. As the time passes, though, you will eventually decide that selling it for whatever you can get, is the only thing left to do.

At that time, you are probably also going to be left with only one group of potential buyers. The neighbors.

53.
What about the original owner?

Now, you might think that the original owner would be a poor choice to sell the property to, but they are actually the best. We sell more back to the original owner than to any other. The price is usually low, but they are sometimes thankful to have the opportunity. Sometimes they are not.

As part of the original title search, you should have located the name and address of the original owner. Sometimes, you can't, and that requires a different track, but sometimes you can use a locating service, and find them even if the county could not. Here you begin to need a more legal knowledge.

To begin with, assuming that the county located the owner and sent the proper notices, you may be surprised to find when you contact the owner, that he has some such excuse as that he just didn't get around to paying the taxes. Many times they know that the property sold, and they didn't hear anything more until they got the final notices. Then they were too unsure about what to do, so they did nothing. This has happened many times. In these circumstances, it seems to be taking advantage of someone to take their property. We usually sell it back to them at a small profit.

Another situation where we find that the original owner was properly notified, but didn't pay, is when they simply could not accumulate sufficient funds. Elderly people, newly divorced women, and those with sudden medical bills easily fall into this category. What you do here, is up to you. You may even give back the property for free.

Then there is the owner who comes to the door with a cigarette and a can of beer, and proceeds to explain how work was slow, they lost their job, or the car broke down. Remember that by this time, they have had well over two years to pay that back tax bill. Here we also sell it back to them. But we make a bigger profit. Can you estimate the annual cost of cigarettes and beer, compared to the property taxes?

There are altogether too many times when the original owner was not totally, or properly notified. Unfortunately, each case is slightly different, but basically, if the property is occupied, the best you can normally hope for is to get your money back with interest. If it is a vacant lot, you may be able to negotiate a slightly larger settlement. Remember that your tax deed, or Clerk's conveyance, is a legal deed unless and until a court decides otherwise. Therefore, it will cost the former owner legal fees and probably your same principal and interest, and possibly your legal fees as well, to reacquire the property. He may negotiate with you.

Lastly, neither you nor the county may have been able to locate the former owner. In this instance, you can file suit to confirm your tax title, or sell the property as-is if it is not worth too much.

54.
Better get a lawyer.

No matter how you arrange the sale, you had better hire an attorney to set the closing, or else depend on the buyer's attorney to handle all the details. BUT. You had better know all of what is going on. Attorneys make mistakes. They can be costly.

By this time, it should be obvious that there are many questions that have a legal bearing on the title to your new property. Locating an attorney is easy. Locating a knowledgeable attorney may not be so easy.

Most attorneys do very little work with tax properties, and usually have a somewhat jaded opinion about them. In every instance, we have had to point them in the proper direction. That is not saying that we know more about the law in general, but only that we do usually know more about the laws that apply to the tax sale than most other people.

Unfortunately, you will either have to trust their judgment and knowledge, or learn the information yourself. The book, "An Introduction to the Mississippi Tax Sale," contains all of this information and has references throughout the book to the appropriate laws and attorney general opinions, which are also included in the back of the book with several cross-reference tables.

It is definitely your best source to search for information about the tax sale. A significant portion of the sales of the book were to attorneys who sought a single comprehensive source to obtain just the information we have been discussing. But it is written for the average person with little technical language. And obviously, I wrote it. Nevertheless, it has been recommended by tax purchasers, Tax Collectors, Chancery Clerks, attorneys, and many others.

There is little that most of us would attempt within the legal system without an attorney, but remember that it is also important to insure that your attorney is well versed in the necessary aspects of the tax sale laws and procedures.

55.
Opinions. Now what?

Most of the properties that forfeit or mature to you, are not
worth a great deal of money. However, even the least
expensive lot may still sell for several hundred dollars. The
biggest problem is that banks will seldom loan money on a
property acquired through a tax deed without either a title
opinion by an attorney, or by having the title confirmed by
the court.

If you have been paying attention, you will have noticed a
new element. In many states, the only method practiced in
the transfer of a title, is normally a review of the title by an
attorney. He then sometimes draws a statement to that effect,
and the deal goes through. If he has made a mistake, either
he or his insurance company will usually correct the problem.

In Mississippi, that is not normally done in solely that
manner. In fact, most attorneys suggest the use of a title
insurance policy, which is simply an additional insurance
coverage.

However, in the case of a tax title, it is normally the
accepted practice to file a suit in court, and to let the court
decide what the title issues might be.

That does not mean that an attorney could not simply
render an opinion, but rather that they generally do not.
There is, however an exception to that. There is a company
in California that will review the procedures and
documentation pertaining to the tax sale, and then if they
approve, they will issue an opinion and there is a title
insurance company that will then immediately issue a policy.
And as the saying goes, "you can take that to the bank."

56.
Let's go to court.

Going to court to perfect the title will likely cost a minimum of a thousand dollars, and usually more. It takes at least six weeks at best, and many have dragged out for a year or more. There is also always the chance that the court will give the property back to the original owner. You may end up losing quite a bit of money.

But it still remains the most viable means of turning a property with only marginally acceptable title into a marketable one. Since it will cost an average of $1,500 or more, it probably does not make much sense to do so where the projected net sales price is not several thousand dollars or more.

Our decision point is around $7,000. If we feel that we can only likely sell a property without a confirmed title, for about $5,000, or less, it does not normally benefit us to confirm it. Therefore, allowing for the extra time and the expenses of doing it, about another two thousand dollars would be necessary to just break even. There are other reasons, such as the property's desirability or lack of it, and the title issues, which greatly affect that decision.

Sometimes, the property may appear to have a substantial value, but title issues may in your opinion, preclude your successful suit to confirm the title. In that circumstance, it may be more sensible to market it as-is, for a much lower price, and let the purchaser assume the risk.

Another possibility with questionable titles, is to simply hold the property for several years, and then to add adverse possession to your suit. That is also something that is very complicated, and definitely needs to be discussed with a knowledgeable attorney. In fact, the whole subject of adverse possession is another of those very misunderstood legal concepts.

Because it happens to be one of the few practical means of acquiring a marketable title when there are some serious deficiencies, we will make an effort to clarify how it is supposed to work. To begin, it is highly difficult to prove all the elements of adverse possession. It requires possession for a period of ten years. It also requires that possession to be exclusive. That is, you must have acted as the sole and undisputed owner for those ten years.

The ten years must have been continuous, and complete, with no break in possession. The possession may have been by someone renting a house, or land from you, and short periods of vacancy may be acceptable. The key is that you must have been in possession and control of the property for the entire ten years.

You must have done so, openly and clearly so that the original owner would have had no doubt but that someone was attempting to usurp his claim to property ownership.

The Mississippi Supreme Court has presented a six point overview that must be met in order for the court to award title based on adverse possession, and you very definitely need to discuss your plan to utilize this method.

The actual Mississippi Code specifically mentions this as a means of perfecting the tax title, and since it may, for various reasons, be the most efficient means of doing so, it is a method that should not be ignored, particularly with those parcels that might have a more significant value, but a questionable title.

Once again though, it is an area that few attorneys are familiar with, and a poorly constructed court suit to confirm title by means of adverse possession, may not succeed due to that lack of competence. Remember. Any attorney may practice law, but that most certainly does not make him an expert in all phases of the law. It does not guarantee him to be even moderately competent in certain areas. You will have to determine this for yourself.

57.
Do it right the first time.

If you do go to court, be certain that you have all of the evidence you need to prove your case. Don't depend on your lawyer. Almost every suit we have reviewed, has had errors. Some of them make you wonder where the lawyer got his license.

According to the Mississippi Supreme Court and the Mississippi Code, there are over twenty separate points that are supposed to be proven or at least averred in every suit to confirm the title to a tax property.

By far, the majority of suits that we have reviewed, have not even attempted to comply with these precepts. When either party is not satisfied with the decision of the Chancery Court, they may bring it before the appellate system.

Many tax purchasers have done so, stating that they believed that the trial court erred. Most of these appeals were so obviously deficient that even a first year law student should have been able to spot the first error. If the owner was not properly notified according to the law, then the court was not only entitled to find for them, but almost required to. Still the tax purchasers ignored this fact and appealed. If the owner was not properly notified, that fact will never get past the appeals process. Never.

So let's get back to the initial point. If you prepare a case to present to court, be absolutely certain that you have everything you need. Here is another point that frequently arises. Present all of your evidence and request several different solutions from the court.

If you don't ask the court to give you back your investment

If it decides against you, then you may not get it back at all, even if you appeal the case. When you appeal, you can not usually present evidence not presented in the original court.

The bottom line remains, do it right and completely, the first time.

58.
If anyone answers, hang up.

You are required to locate and notify the person who lost the property and make him a defendant in your case. If he answers the suit, with a reasonable defense, forget it. The court will find for him. As soon as a defendant answers, your case is probably lost, so think about quitting before it costs any more money. Discuss this thoroughly with your attorney.

Many times, the defendant will be a lienholder who was properly notified. When they receive the summons, they turn it over to their lawyers who file a standard 'we deny everything' answer. In this event, if you assemble all of your evidence that they were properly noticed and who signed for the notice, etc., you may contact the attorney and discuss the matter. Normally, if you are polite but determined, and explain the notification requirements, and offer to fax them a copy of the signed receipt, they will agree to review that and get back to you. Give them a few days, and then contact them and politely request them to either file an amended answer, or to give you a quitclaim deed.

If you have done your homework and the correct procedures have been followed, most lienholders can be made to go away.

Almost without exception, at least some errors have been made in the notification process. If the original owner contests the suit, his lawyer will usually have several issues that he will bring before the court to try to dispute your claim to the property.

In this type of suit, it is the duty of the court to find for the former owner unless you can prove compliance with almost all of the rules and procedures. In other words, the court will have a bias towards the original owner. And it is very unlikely that all of the rules will have been followed correctly. So you will lose.

Our policy is to thoroughly review the notices before filing the suit. Sometimes there is a question that may be decided by the court. If the circumstances appear to warrant it, we will then file the suit. If no one answers, then the court may find in our favor.

But if the former owner answers the suit, and there is a question as to the proper notification or some other factor, then we will attempt to negotiate out of court. This is to both parties' advantage since legal expenses may add up very quickly. It normally costs at least a thousand dollars just for the preparation work. Every day in court just adds more.

There is some question of negligence which may be applied, and which might allow you to recoup legal expenses, but don't count on it. This issue has not gone through the appellate process and is still decided by the local trial court.

The bottom line here is that if someone answers, in most cases, it is better to negotiate and attempt to settle out of court. Obviously, this must be decided on a case by case basis, and depends on too many factors to determine here. Discuss this thoroughly with your attorney. It is also sensible to have an understanding ahead of time, about what the expenses will be if someone answers the suit versus obtaining a default judgment.

As long ago as the Bible and before, there was a good bit of advice. Settle out of court.

59.
Judgment day. [You hope]

Eventually, if no one answers, your attorney will ask the court for a paper that says that the court agrees that you own the property. When this is filed, you are officially the owner. Now there are a number of exceptions to this, so be certain to question your attorney.

Essentially, if no one has answered after a period of thirty days has passed from the time they were notified, your attorney will draw a paper for the court to sign. That will be what is called a default judgment. It merely states that by reason of no one having disagreed with you, the court finds for you in your suit. Usually this contains many false suppositions, and errors, but it is normally accepted by the court and the people who read it afterward.

In the event that someone answers your suit, but cannot prove his point, the court may issue a judgment in your favor in the same manner. This will likely be a declaratory or a summary judgment. This judgment is more likely to be appealed, but is also more likely to be upheld in appeal because the Chancery Court makes few errors when evidence is presented to it, as is the case in both these types of judgments.

When one of the many errors occurs with a default judgment, a defendant who for a legitimate reason, did not answer, may later convince the court to overturn the judgment. Or the process may go to appeal, where it almost always will be overturned due to those errors.

60.
Don't forget policy.

As soon as you get a judgment filed, don't forget to get a title insurance policy from your attorney. If you have gone to the trouble and expense of confirming the title, it only makes very good sense to get that policy.

People have said that it didn't make sense because they already had a judgment by the court saying that they had complete title. Unfortunately, there are many cases where the judgment did not include certain heirs or lienholders even though they were locatable or recorded. Guess what happened to the judgment.

Another point here is that even though you may have a very good claim, supported by a judgment, it does not prevent the other party from filing suit to reclaim some supposed rights. You will then have to pay the legal expenses to contest their allegations. It only takes one suit like that to pay for a number of title insurance policies. Remember, if someone contests your claim to the title, the insurance company will either provide legal counsel or settle with the other people, or pay you the amount of your loss.

Sometimes it may not seem to be necessary, but that is a decision for you to make.

61.
It's developing nicely.

Many times, it is more suitable to do something with the property rather than just selling it. A few acres might change into a small subdivision or shopping area. You might build a house on a vacant lot. Many developed properties are much easier to sell than raw land.

Another factor is what we call legitimizing the value. Let's take a vacant lot for example. It may have a value from a few hundred dollars to many thousands. How do you set a price? More importantly, how do you convince others of its value?

Well, that lot will be a part of the sale price of any house built on it. Most appraisers have little or no real knowledge of property construction costs. Whenever one uses the term 'cost per square foot,' you can forget the remainder of what he says. No competent estimator would ever calculate construction costs in that manner.

However, another factor that normally gets into the appraisal is that of assuming the value of the lot to be about 15 to 25 percent of the total price. With this in mind, a house that costs a hundred thousand dollars to build, would probably sell for about $140,000, allowing for a profit and the cost of the land. This would give a value to the lot of about $25,000.

Moreover, if the house sells at a profit, you could then also pocket the entire difference between your cost and the $25,000. On the other hand, if you sold just the lot, a person might not want to pay top dollar for it, and might even object to its being worth anything even near that price.

Of course, changing or enhancing the value of a property might be even more lucrative on larger scale projects. Developing raw acreage into a finished commercial property can result in huge increases in the value of the underlying land.

One of the important points in valuing any property is to explore its greatest potential use. Unfortunately, it may take a long time to locate someone who agrees, and is willing to purchase the property for that particular type of project. At times, it may be to your advantage to pursue that avenue yourself.

Another advantage at that point is to be able to use your presumed equity in that land as part of the financing package, thus again legitimizing its value.

62.
Now for the sharks.

There are two kinds of sharks in this business. Most people seem to have heard that a tax title is not any good. At least that is what they say when they want to buy the property from you. As soon as they buy it, they begin to brag about how good a deal they got. The only answer is to set a legitimate price, taking into consideration how good the title seems to be, and what its best use value might be. Then stick with that price or lower it only if you are convinced that it will not sell otherwise.

Then there is the other type of shark. And that can get you into trouble. You may have a piece of land for sale with an almost definitely bad title, but still attempt to sell it for a high price. There are laws to prevent that sort of thing, and you might find yourself in serious trouble if you do.

Much of what matures to us, is of very little value. It may be just a ditch, or a very irregular shaped lot, or it might have a title that has no possibility of being perfected. That is simply the expected outcome of the sale. Most of us attempt to negotiate it back to the original owner, or simply let it go for taxes the next year. It's just part of the game.

63.
Tell it like it is.

We have always tried to tell people everything we know about what we are selling. No matter what you may think, we have always found this to be the best policy. Word gets around. People will find out things from someone. They really appreciate finding out from you first. If a property has some defects, tell the potential buyer. If he doesn't buy it, he may end up selling it for you to someone else.

Many people have purchased more than one property from us. They were very satisfied with the first one, and then for various reasons, bought another. Many others have had a relative or friend that also bought from us. It is very difficult to build that type of reputation, but very easy to lose it.

Another point here lies with the various real estate and consumer protection laws. If you knowingly fail to disclose certain detrimental information, you may be in violation of a number of laws. Check with your attorney,

64.
The fine print. [Theirs and yours]

Whenever you sign a purchase offer or a deed, read the whole thing. No matter how many times you have heard that, remember it this time. There is usually something wrong with almost every prepared document. Sometimes it can be very expensive and annoying to correct.

Because we deal with tax properties, there is even more of a chance that the standard purchase offer will have portions that do not apply. If you deal with a real estate broker, talk it over and get them to use a form that suits you, or be prepared to draw through the standard form, and insert your own clauses. Here again, legal advice is going to be almost a necessity.

Perhaps the biggest difficulty will be to overcome the misguided interpretation that you need to sell a property with a warranty deed. You do not. We sell almost everything on a quitclaim deed. In fact, there is probably no instance that I can think of that would require a warranty deed, yet many attorneys will counsel their clients not to accept a transfer on a quitclaim deed. Sometimes they can be educated, but not often. However, you can never sell a tax property that has not had its title confirmed, on a warranty deed..

I have written articles on this subject, but there is only a very slow acceptance of the idea. Briefly, though, a warranty deed does just that. It warrants or guarantees that the title to the property is perfectly good, or you will do whatever it takes to make it good. Do you really want to give yourself that responsibility?

Consider, for instance the house where you live. If you sold it, you would probably be purchasing another with the proceeds. Remember though, that over many years, we have found that about half of the deeds had errors. Usually they are minor, but not always. Would you like to be responsible for making the title good on a house of the value of yours?

On the other hand, a quitclaim deed transfers title quite satisfactorily, but does not guarantee it. Many attorneys will point to a title insurance policy and say that if you have one, then it will cover you for your title error. I tell them back that if that is so, then get the buyer to purchase one. The fact remains that we have had cases drag on for well over a year before the title company settled. Once again. Most attorneys are used to warranty deeds, but you do what seems best to you. Here is also where you need to locate an attorney for your work, who understands and accepts the use of quitclaim deeds.

65.
Your hot little hands.
[not till it's there]

So many times we thought for sure that someone was going to buy something. It almost seems that whenever a deal is pending, something will foul it up if you are counting too much on it. Play it cool right up to the time you cash the check. Then you can celebrate. Most property sales do not take place on the first opportunity. Sometimes there is no actual purchase offer made. Sometimes people can't get financing. Sometimes they just change their minds.

On one deal, the buyer was ready. The financing was in place. The appraisal was satisfactory. A closing was set for two days away. The bank backed out. Then they did another appraisal. It was also satisfactory. This went on for several weeks. Eventually, it did sell, but not until five separate closings were proposed.

Alternatively, dozens of times, the deal has fallen through. Sometimes the buyer just gets 'cold feet.' Sometimes there is a last minute problem with financing. But frequently the property doesn't sell without some setback in the original arrangements.

If you handle the closing yourself, there is one more important point. CASH. Many times, with the sale of cheap properties, the purchaser brings a check. NO. The wording of the deed, which you sign and have notarized, plainly states that you are transferring the property after having been properly and completely paid or with a mortgage. If you so state, then it may be perjury to later attempt to collect on a bad check. You may have to go to court to overturn your deed. The judge is not going to appreciate your wasting his time with your mistakes. Guess what he might do. Take only cash or a cashier's check.

66.
Charts and things.

If you purchase very many tax certificates, you will probably find it much easier to keep track of the results by putting the information into the computer. A spreadsheet becomes a very useful tool for reviewing and comparing data. Some people will want to produce charts or graphs to show the data.

Interest rates of return, annual income, and many other calculations are much easier on a computer. Most computers either come with a spreadsheet program, or one can be purchased or even downloaded free off the internet.

The more tax certificates you purchase, the more important it becomes to be able to analyze and compare information. And if you continue with this excellent investment, year to year comparisons are also quite useful.

Finally, you may have seen others at the tax sale, who had data sheets instead of the newspaper. You can purchase this information and print it from your computer. A good example of how useful those data sheets can be, occurred during this year's sale. The Tax Collector called a number and while everyone was turning the page of the newspaper and looking for that next parcel, we already located it and got the bid on a $20,000 certificate for only the taxes. Most of the large taxes receive several percent overbids, but because everyone else was distracted by the attempts to locate that particular parcel in the paper, we saved several thousand dollars.

67.
What taxes?

Keep in mind that the property you acquire through the tax sale, will sell each year and by the end of your first year, it will mature to the next purchaser unless you redeem at least that next year. This will continue each year until you pay the taxes up to date, or sell the property.

This is one of those very difficult to understand portions of the tax sale process. Let's review how the sale is supposed to work. The person who is the registered owner of a parcel on January first of a year, is the one who is taxed. But the tax bill is not sent until the last few weeks of that year. The owner has until February 1st of the next year to pay those taxes without interest or penalty.

After that, interest is added each month that the taxes remain unpaid. This continues until either the first Monday in April, or, in most counties, until the last Monday in August. Then the property is sold to the highest bidder.

The new purchaser however, can not do anything with the property for a period of two years. During that time, the original owner has complete right of possession, and may redeem the property at any time.

After the first tax sale, the original owner continues to receive annual tax bills. But the taxes must be paid in sequential order. Therefor, before being able to pay a more current tax, the prior years' tax bills must be paid.

The first result of this is that unless the back taxes were paid, the current year's can not be paid by Feb 1st. The property will then sell again the next year. This will continue each year until someone redeems the property.

The person who first purchased it at the tax sale, will have it forfeit to him at the end of two years. But that becomes retroactive back to the day it was purchased. That purchaser now owns the property, but remember, it has also sold one time since he purchased it, and will sell again at the tax sale for that year, at about the time that it forfeits.

The person who purchased it at the second tax sale, has now owned his rights to it for a period of one year. If the person who purchased it two years ago, (and is now the owner) does not redeem the taxes, then in one more year, it will fully mature to that second purchaser.

The result of this process is that the tax purchaser who buys at a sale and then acquires the property, has also had it sell to someone else, and it will forfeit to those successive purchasers unless the taxes are redeemed.

By paying all of the back taxes, and keeping them paid to date, then that will eliminate this problem.

This is probably the most difficult concept about the tax sale to understand. Other points may be misunderstood, or have incorrect interpretations, but there is a basic and fairly clear cut underlying set of laws that apply. And once a person delves into those rules, it begins to make reasonable sense. This particular procedure is more confusing though, and there is no separate law that seems to adequately clarify it. Just take it for granted that you will lose a property if you don't pay the taxes before the expiration of its next forfeiture date.

And one thing more. Remember that the date that the tax sale matures will be different each year, and will not be the same date as the tax sale that year. This is extremely important, because if you wait until the tax sale date, it might be too late to redeem. After the close of business on the 2nd anniversary of the tax sale, the county may no longer accept payments for redemptions for that year. You will have lost the property to the next purchaser.

There is another point to discuss here, and that is the fact that as the owner, you may only be deprived of your ownership if you are properly notified, just as the original owner was supposed to have been. There are two aspects to this. First of all, remember that most tax sale notices are not properly and completely delivered. That may present you with a chance to rescue your claim if it is accidentally lost due to your not paying those taxes.

The other side of that lies with the understanding that you are a knowledgeable and sophisticated investor. Don't depend on the court agreeing with your whining that you were not properly notified. It would be very easy for the court to decide that your original claim was not any good either. As usual, be careful of what you say.

68.
More taxes?

Don't forget that you will have to pay taxes on the profit from the sale of the property you get at the tax sale. Although there may be a good tax break on your federal taxes, the state may cost you a lot more.

The government calls the profit or loss from the sale of real property, a capital gain or loss. Under the present tax structure this results in usually a much lower or even no tax at all.

Unfortunately, the State of Mississippi does not presently give such large tax breaks to persons who sell properties at a profit. For most people, their federal tax is much higher than their state tax. In this instance, though, the portion of those taxes devoted to the profit from the sale of real estate, is frequently much higher for the state than that of the federal income tax. In fact, for many purchasers, there is no federal tax on the sale of property.

Since the tax laws change periodically, it would be important to have a more thorough understanding of them, and/or to consult with both an attorney and an accountant.

69.
Are we done yet?

The days pass and we hope to get rid of all of our newly acquired real estate. We may try to do it ourselves, or use a broker. We may try newspaper ads, signs on the property, letters and sometimes telephone calls. We may try contacting the neighbors in person. We may try to develop the land for a better use.

We may attempt to confirm the title, or we may decide to sell it as-is. Sometimes we will pay the taxes and keep it another year. Sometimes we will decide that the property has good potential, but that it may take a longer period to sell it.

Finally, you will either sell the property, or lose it to the next tax purchaser. All of the research and investigating and bidding and collating data, and marketing are done. Now you can relax.

70.
Don't just sit there.

Perhaps the most debilitating disease known to progress is procrastination. By the time you realize that a property has forfeited to you, there is less than a year before it will accrue to someone else if you do not pay the taxes. That should be plenty of time to proceed with a well organized plan to dispose of your holdings. It almost never happens. For whatever reason, properties are lost, or we pay taxes on them for several years before getting rid of them. Jump on the project and keep it moving. It's your money.

Now, it is almost a sure bet that the vast majority of readers will look at this and say, "That's not going to be me." On the other hand, the remainder of the bet is that, yes it will. Prove it to yourself. Next year, analyze what you have or have not done as a result of the tax sale. Procrastination? I hope you can honestly say that you were found not guilty

71.
Not again!

Of course, for most of us in this business, when things begin to settle down, and we have sold most of our properties, it is time for the next sale, and we start all over again.

If you plan to invest over a long period of time, as most people do, who have been introduced to the tax sale, it begins to become obvious that certain parcels sell every year. Others seem to be redeemed very early in the process, while still others may not be redeemed until the last minute.

And, as the focus of most of this book, there are normally from a few to several hundred that forfeit to the tax purchaser each year. Over many years, we have developed several strategies to increase either our interest return or the number of properties that matured to us.

Some strategies work well. Others are greatly affected by such things as hurricanes. Here, this book is laying the ground work for you to be able to have a better understanding about how the tax sale is supposed to work, and how it actually does. It is not intended to provide information about how to purchase the parcels, but only about what happens after the sale.

As you deal with the issues over the year, some sort of strategy or procedure may occur to you. Test it out. Check it against what data you have. Our one suggestion here is to obtain as much current and past information as you can, and attempt to divine some order or theory that appears to hold a chance for a better return for your money. Remember though, people have always invented theories and schemes that supposedly produced more money. They seldom work.

Much, much more.

Of course, there is a great deal more to know about the tax sale. As an investment, it probably offers one of the best opportunities for most people to earn a good rate of return with a very low risk. But like most investments, it is wise to know as much as possible about your endeavors. Having a more complete knowledge can only help to better guide you in making investment decisions.

This book has been an attempt to give a fair grounding in the actions that take place following the tax sale. It is written in a light manner, with little need for complex study. Yet it should provide answers and suggestions to cover most situations arising subsequent to the sale. Most people will find at least some points that will possibly clarify issues that had been confusing.

One point that always arises with some readers of my books, is that of the "that's not the way we do it, and I've been working here for 20 years," syndrome. Unfortunately, no matter how well you attempt to educate people, many will still remain with past beliefs. The phrase, "my mind's made up, don't confuse me with the facts," seems made to order.

Attempting to deal with those people is probably a lost cause. However, we have had at least occasional success by pointing to the appropriate Mississippi Attorney General's opinion, or to the section of the Mississippi Code that applies.

When you do encounter such issue conflicts, the A G opinions and the Mississippi Code are located online at their websites. By using the search procedure, most subjects can be located fairly quickly, and a printed copy will at least provide you with the proof or denial of your understanding.

And to repeat, the book, "An Introduction to the Mississippi Tax Sale," is available online, and is the best source of complete information about how the tax sale functions. It is written for everyone in non-technical language, and includes references to the applicable laws and even includes those laws for additional reference.

Good luck, and good investing.